# A Reading Skillbuilder

## Lesson Plans, Ideas and Activities for Teaching Comprehension Skills

# A Reading Skillbuilder

Lesson Plans, Ideas and Activities for Teaching Comprehension Skills

Harry W. Forgan

Illustrations by
Bonnie Flint Striebel

**Scott, Foresman and Company**
Glenview, Illinois
Dallas, TX   Oakland, NJ   Palo Alto, CA   Tucker, GA   London, England

Printed in the United States of America

ISBN:   0-673-16549-3

2345678910-MAL-89878685848382

To Chuck McDermott, my "buddy teacher" and
great friend. I am grateful for his advice when I
was a beginning teacher and for his witty
character, which provides us with so
many laughs and enjoyable times.

# Contents

# Preface

The lesson plans in this book are in a ready-to-use format. Teachers are encouraged to adapt the lesson plans to go along with their teaching styles and the needs of the children. For each lesson plan, you will find a specific objective, the suggested instructional reading level at which the plan will be most effective, materials needed, detailed instructional procedures, two practice activities, and tips for teaching related lessons.

There are three ready-to-duplicate activity sheets to accompany each lesson plan. First, there is a Lesson Activity Sheet that can be used with the children while you are teaching the lesson. Second, there is a Practice Activity Sheet that provides an opportunity for the children to use the skill after it has been introduced. Third, there is a Home Activity Sheet that can be used as homework to involve parents in helping their children learn to read.

You will be able to use the final section of each lesson plan titled "Tips for Teaching Related Lessons" as a resource many times after you have taught the introductory lesson. This section provides practical information on other objectives to teach and additional teaching techniques.

My hope is that these ideas will stimulate your thinking as you increase your expertise as a reading teacher. I know that many teachers get additional ideas when they look at someone else's plans and adapt these ideas to their own teaching styles. You will notice that the lesson plans are not presented in a verbatim format, but rather, step by step procedures are described in a logical sequence. You will make these lesson plans come alive as you implement them with children.

Several people helped me to write this book. Carole Bernstein compiled some of the lists of words that are used with the tips for teaching related lessons. My family has also been most understanding and supportive. Jimmy, now a teenager, and Jennifer, age 8, have kept me young and in good spirits. It has been a pleasure to see them learn to read. Ruth Ann, my wife, has graciously typed many drafts of the various lesson plans in addition to the final copy. She is encouraging and helps me keep my daily activities in a balanced perspective. I would not be able to share my ideas if I did not have the love and confidence of my family.

I would like to extend a special word of appreciation to Bonnie Striebel who prepared all of the illustrations for this book. I truly believe her illustrations make my ideas come alive.

# Introduction

## How This Book Can Help You

Children are not really reading unless they are getting meaning as they read. The eight lesson plans in this book are designed to help you facilitate children's comprehension abilities. Separate lesson plans are provided to help you teach children to note the significant details, the main idea, and the sequence of events. You will want children to draw conclusions and to evaluate critically as they read, so model lesson plans for these two skills are provided. The essence of comprehension is vocabulary. One area of expertise that you implement every day is that of helping children learn the meanings of words. The model lesson plan for vocabulary development includes many ideas that you can use to help children increase their vocabularies. The lesson plans for oral reading and rate of comprehension will provide you with techniques for enabling children to develop those critical skills.

In summary, this book provides many exciting ideas for teacher-directed lessons. Rather than telling children to do particular assignments, the emphasis is on explaining, clarifying, and extending the skills that must be developed in order to read effectively. I believe you will enjoy reading the ideas and adapting them and using materials in your own way. Let us take a closer look now at the format of each lesson plan and special tips for adapting these plans for your purposes and teaching style.

## The Format of the Model Lesson Plans

Each of the model lesson plans in this book follows the same format. First, the specific objective is indicated. Second, the instructional reading level for which the objective is most appropriate is specified. If there is a prerequisite reading level that the children should have before completing the lesson plan, it is summarized in the section titled "Instruc-

tional Reading Level." Next you will find a list of materials that are needed to use the lesson plan. In every lesson plan there are ready-to-reproduce materials. The Lesson Activity Sheet can be used as you conduct the teacher-directed lesson. The Practice Activity Sheet is designed for children to use after your instruction. Finally, there is a Home Activity Sheet designed to be done as homework. If other materials are necessary, they are listed in the third section of the lesson plan.

The heart of the lesson plan consists of the instructional procedures, which are numbered for convenience. As you prepare to use the lesson plan, you are encouraged to read through the instructional procedures and decide how you want to proceed. You should use these plans in a flexible manner depending on the responses of the children. In developing the lesson plans, I tried to anticipate a wide range of responses and provide for them. At the same time, I realize that it is impossible to anticipate every response the children will make. I believe you will find the instructional procedures and the method of presenting them both stimulating and flexible.

The next part of the lesson plan is called practice. Here is where you will find a description of how to use the Practice Activity Sheet and the Home Activity Sheet that accompany each lesson. I realize that children need more than one practice activity, but within the limits of one book it was not possible to provide all the practice activities they need. I would refer you to *The Reading Corner* (Goodyear, 1977), my companion textbook, for additional practice activities.

The last part of the lesson plan may be one of the most important because it deals with tips for teaching related lessons. Here you will find additional objectives related to the major objective, as well as advice on how to teach and/or provide practice ac-

tivities. You will refer to "Tips for Teaching Related Lessons" many times because it is designed to extend and expand the model lesson plan.

As you examine the lesson plans, you will notice that some basic principles of instruction are implemented in every lesson. First, I believe it is important for children to understand why they are learning particular skills. At the beginning of every lesson plan, you will find ideas for helping children understand the new skill they are expected to learn and why they are expected to learn it. The children will discover how this new skill will help them become better readers. Second, as you examine the lesson plans, you will find that the instructional procedures are "snappy" and lively. Teachers must be able to get and maintain the attention of students if instruction is to be effective. The lesson plans generally take from ten to thirty minutes depending on the grade level of the children. Another aspect of the lesson plans is the inclusion of ideas for clarifying and explaining. Finally, you will note the importance of praise and positive, immediate reinforcement.

**Guidelines for Using the Lesson Plans**

In preparing to use a particular lesson plan, your first step is to identify the skills your students need.

Even though you may be a third grade teacher, you will be teaching some first grade reading skills as well as some that are used in the fifth grade because of the individual differences of your students.

After you have identified a particular objective or skill area that is appropriate for some of your students, you can use the book to locate a model lesson plan for that skill area. You should begin by noting the specific objective and the instructional reading level that is suggested for the lesson plan. After doing so, you will find a list of the materials. Take time to examine the Lesson Activity Sheet, the Practice Activity Sheet, and the Home Activity Sheet that accompany each lesson plan. As you read the detailed instructional procedures, you will learn how to introduce the lesson and how to use the Lesson Activity Sheet during the lesson. You can make notes about how you want to proceed as you read the suggested procedures. Finally, read the ideas for introducing the Practice Activity Sheet and the Home Activity Sheet that are designed to be used to practice and apply the reading skill.

There are several ways to prepare the reproducible materials. Frequently, teachers like to make a thermofax master of the Lesson Activity Sheet, the Practice Activity Sheet, and the Home Activity Sheet so each child can be provided with a copy. If

you want to adapt these materials in any way, it is best to do so before making thermofax masters. To make a thermofax master, you need special thermofax material and access to a thermofax machine. This procedure is economical because you simply put the page that you want copied in the thermofax master and run it through the thermofax machine. Within a few seconds, you have a master from which you can duplicate many copies.

If the paper supply in your school is limited, you may want to make a transparency of the Lesson Activity Sheet to use in the overhead projector as you conduct the lesson. You can also laminate the Practice Activity Sheet and make one durable copy available to the students. I would suggest making a copy of the Home Activity Sheet for every child if at all possible. Please do not feel that the parents of your students are not willing to help until you have tried many different techniques to get them involved. You may want to use the sample letter that I have included for parents. Feel free to adapt the letter in any way or to use it as is. Learning to read is greatly fostered when home and school work together.

Dear Parents,

I am writing to you to ask you to help your child practice some of the reading skills we are working on this year. Reading is a skill, and as with other skills, such as playing the piano, practice is necessary to become excellent. I will be providing some practice work at school. However, I believe that your child will be even more successful if the reading skills are practiced at home.

I believe that you and your child will enjoy the practice work that I will send home. The Home Activity Sheets are homework sheets that your child can do with very little assistance from you. These activities do not require you to turn your home into a miniature school. Because children like to please their parents, it is important for you to read the notes from me and talk about the work with your child.

Helping your child can be a very pleasant experience if you praise the child and remember to have patience, because learning takes time. Your child wants to do well when working with you and feels upset when you are angry and/or disappointed. Be sure to point out the good things your child is able to do and stop working with the child if the material is too difficult. Rather than becoming extremely upset with your child, write me a note saying that your child doesn't understand the assignment.

The first Home Activity Sheet is attached to this letter. I hope that you and your child enjoy doing it.

# Teaching Comprehension Skills

Significant Details
Main Idea
Sequence of Events
Drawing Conclusions
Evaluating Critically
Vocabulary Development
Rates of Comprehension
Oral Reading

# Significant Details

**SPECIFIC OBJECTIVE**

The children will be able to create visual images by noting significant details as they read.

**INSTRUCTIONAL READING LEVEL**

1/1-1/2. Even though this model lesson plan is intended for children with first grade instructional reading levels, there are children at higher instructional reading levels who still have difficulty noticing significant details. The materials in this lesson can be adapted to higher instructional reading levels.

**MATERIALS**

1. The "Reading Is Like Making a Picture" Lesson Activity Sheet
2. The "My Filmstrip" Practice Activity Sheet
3. The "Fill in the Facts" Home Activity Sheet

**INSTRUCTIONAL PROCEDURES**

1. Begin this lesson by telling the children that when they read, they are really making a picture. The same thing is true if somebody reads to them. Tell the children to close their eyes as you tell them a story. As you tell them the story, you want them to try to make a picture in their minds of what they hear. Tell the children one of their favorite stories such as "The Three Little Pigs," "Little Red Riding Hood," "Jack and the Beanstalk," "Goldilocks and the Three Bears," or another favorite old tale. After doing so, have the children describe some of the pictures they have made in their minds. Ask them what kind of shirt Jack had on in the story "Jack and the Beanstalk," or what kind of shoes Goldilocks was wearing. Tell them that as they listen to someone read or tell a story, and when they themselves read, they are making a picture.

2. Give the children a copy of the "Reading Is Like Making a Picture" Lesson Activity Sheet. Have the children read the story with you and again ask them to try to make a picture of what they have read. As the children read the story, have them use their crayons to complete the pictures by illustrating the details in the story. Supervise the children's drawings to see if they are making their pictures according to the facts that were presented in the story.

3. Summarize this lesson by telling the children that when we read, we are really trying to make a picture show or television program. In lessons that follow, continually ask the children to create visual images as they read.

**PRACTICE**

1. Give the children a copy of the "My Filmstrip" Practice Activity Sheet. Tell the children that they are going to be able to make their own filmstrip. Have the children notice that the filmstrip on the Lesson Activity Sheet needs to be colored to make it more attractive. Ask the children to read the story and color the filmstrip to show what the story says. In doing so, the children will be required to read details and then illustrate the details in the pictures on the filmstrip.

2. Tell the children you have a letter for their parents that includes a story without any details. The story is to be all about each child. Tell the children that you want them to sit down with their parents and have the parents write in the facts. When the children bring their stories back to school, provide opportunities for them to share with each other. In doing so, the children will be seeing how details make stories interesting.

**TIPS FOR TEACHING RELATED LESSONS**

1. When reading with the children, ask them to identify the most important details in various sentences. After they have done so, ask them why they feel these details are so important. Remember, their

responses might vary depending on the background of experiences each child brings to the story.

2. Provide easy-to-read stories from children's magazines such as *Ebony Jr.*, *Highlights*, or *Sesame Street* and ask the children to circle the details they believe are most important. After doing so, have the children share the magazines with each other and pay attention to the details as they create their own mental pictures.

3. Ask the children to draw a picture of one of their favorite paragraphs or parts of the story. In doing so, the children should try to make their picture just like the details described in the paragraph or story.

**ACTIVITY SHEET DIRECTIONS**
**Reading Is Like Making a Picture (page 4)**

Read the story on the Lesson Activity Sheet with the children. Ask them to complete and color the pictures to correspond with the story.

**My Filmstrip (page 5)**

Direct the students to look at the pictures on the Practice Activity Sheet and then read the sentences next to each picture. They should color the pictures using the colors mentioned in the sentences. When they are finished, they will have used five different colors. Remind them that reading is like making a picture.

# Reading Is Like Making a Picture

Hi! My name is Ann.

I am six years old.

Today is my birthday.

I am wearing my pink party dress.

My hair is brown.

I got a puppy today.

I call her Spot.

She is black.

She has some white spots.

Spot likes to play.

She likes to chase the red ball.

The red ball is under the table.

Spot likes to drink water.

Her bowl has two sides.

I put water in one side.

I put food in the other side.

There is a hotdog in her dish.

I cut the hotdog into three pieces.

From *A Reading Skillbuilder: Comprehension* © 1982 by Scott, Foresman & Co. Harry W. Forgan and Bonnie F. Striebel

# My Filmstrip

This is my dog. He is brown.

My dog wears a yellow shirt.

My dog has a green dish.

I feed my dog red dog food.

I put my dog's purple collar on to take him for a walk.

From *A Reading Skillbuilder: Comprehension* © 1982 by Scott, Foresman & Co.
Harry W. Forgan and Bonnie F. Striebel

NAME_____DATE_____

# Fill in the Facts

Dear Parents,

My teacher is teaching me how to notice the most important facts when I read. She says that when I am reading, I am really making a picture. For example, when I read the sentence, "The dog has a green dish," I can think of what the dog looks like and see the green dish.

My teacher says the facts in the story make the story interesting. If a story doesn't have many facts, it isn't very interesting. My teacher says we can write an interesting story with a lot of facts about me. Can you write in the facts I tell you? When I go to school I will read this story to others.

From *A Reading Skillbuilder: Comprehension* © 1982 by Scott, Foresman & Co. Harry W. Forgan and Bonnie F. Striebel

There is a _____ named _____. _____ is _____ years old.

_____ was born on _____ in _____. There are _____ people in

_____ family. _____ likes to watch _____ on television.

_____ likes to read books about _____. _____ favorite

foods are _____ and _____. _____ likes to play _____.

_____ likes to collect _____. _____ gets up at

_____ and goes to bed at _____.

# Main Idea

## SPECIFIC OBJECTIVE

The children will be able to find the commonality among details and state the main idea of a paragraph.

## INSTRUCTIONAL READING LEVEL

2/1–2/2. Even though this model lesson plan is designed for use with children who have a second grade instructional level, there are some children who are at higher levels and need instruction concerning how to find the main idea. You can adapt the suggestions in this lesson plan using higher level instructional reading materials.

## MATERIALS

1. The "How Are We Alike?" Lesson Activity Sheet
2. The "I Have the Main Idea — In My Hand!" Practice Activity Sheet
3. The "Stick to the Topic" Home Activity Sheet

## INSTRUCTIONAL PROCEDURES

1. Begin this lesson by telling the children that when we read we always want to know what we are reading about. We want to find the most important ideas because this helps us understand what we read. Tell the children that you are going to teach them how to find the most important idea — or the main idea — so they will understand what they read.

2. Give each child a copy of the "How Are We Alike" Lesson Activity Sheet. Direct the children's attention to the first row and have them look at the words on each of the fingers on the first hand. Read the words to them and have them try to guess how all of these words are alike. Read peanut butter and jelly, bologna, BLT (bacon, lettuce, and tomato), ham, and cheese. If the children do not understand that all of the words are sandwiches, tell them. Write the word *sandwiches* on the board and have the children write it on the palm of the hand on their paper. Tell the children that you want them to write the word *sandwiches* on the palm of the hand because all of these words are types of sandwiches.

3. Have the children find the second hand in the first row. Ask them to read the words that are on the fingers. Ask them how a chair, a desk, a couch, a bed, and a dresser are alike. The children should be able to tell you that the items are furniture. Some of the children may identify the items as things you find in your house. Accept this answer, but probe a little further to find out what these things would be called. If they do not say "furniture," ask them what kind of a store you would go to to buy these things. Direct the children to write the word *furniture* on the palm of the hand because all of these words name furniture.

4. Now direct the children's attention to the last hand in the row. Have them notice that the palm of the hand says *colors*. Ask the children what they could write on the fingers to tell about colors. As they name various colors, write them on the board and have the children write the names of the colors on the fingers.

5. Tell the children to look at the center part of the page. Tell them that on the fingers of this hand there is a short story. Ask each child in turn to read a sentence and to think about a good name for the story. Then ask the children to reread the sentences to find out how all of them are alike:

    a. Jimmy and Jenny went on a trip.
    b. They went with their parents.
    c. They stayed in a motel.
    d. Every day they went swimming.
    e. They played games and read in the evening.

Ask the children to tell you what all of these sentences tell about. (Jimmy and Jenny's vacation trip). If the children cannot state the main idea, go through each sentence to see what it tells about. Point out that each sentence tells about what Jimmy and Jenny did on vacation. After the children have arrived at the main idea, such as "Jimmy and Jenny's Trip" or a related title, have them write it on the palm of the hand. If the children say, for example, that a good title is "Fun at the Motel," help them to realize that this is not the best title because every sentence does not apply to that title. Continue to probe until the children examine *each* sentence and state a title that tells about all of them.

6. Now direct the children's attention to the last row on the page. Have them read the title on the palm, "Dogs Are Man's Best Friends." Ask the children what they might read if they were reading a story that tells about dogs as man's best friends. Begin by asking the children why some people think a dog is man's best friend. The children might point out facts such as dogs never get angry with you, dogs are fun to play with, dogs protect people, dogs like to show affection, and dogs like to please their masters by obeying. After the children share some of their ideas, write each one on the chalkboard and then have the children write them or key words on each one of the fingers. When the children are all done, help them to see that their sentences tell about the main idea, "Dogs Are Man's Best Friends."

7. Summarize the lesson by telling the children that as they are reading they should be thinking about how all of the details or facts are alike. When they understand how they are alike, they will know the main idea and will thus be able to better understand what they read.

## PRACTICE

1. Give the children a copy of the "I Have the Main Idea — In My Hand" Practice Activity Sheet. Tell the children you have a story for them to read. After they read the story, they should trace one of their hands. After tracing their hands, the children should write a fact or a detail on each one of the fingers. They can then read the facts and try to figure out how all of them are alike. After they do so, they should write the main idea on the palm of the hand they have drawn. When the children have completed their work, have them bring it to the reading circle to share the details they found and how they think all of the details are alike. The children should be able to state that the main idea tells about the time the hamster escaped from his cage.

2. Tell the children you would like them to work with their parents to make a booklet about one topic. Tell them you are sending a letter home to their parents that gives them some topics such as "My

Wish Book" or "Foods I Like to Eat." Tell the children they will be cutting out pictures from newspapers or old magazines for their booklets. Remind the children to stick to one topic and only include pictures about the topic in their booklet. If they want to make two or three booklets, they are welcome to do so, but the pictures in one booklet should be about the same topic. Ask the children to bring their completed booklets to school to show the others. When they share their booklets, their classmates must guess what the title of the booklet is.

## TIPS FOR TEACHING RELATED LESSONS

1. When you are working with the children in a reading group, ask them to state the main idea of different paragraphs in the story. Write each of the main ideas on the board. Now have the children examine all of the main ideas of the paragraphs to determine the main idea of the story. Again, they will be looking for commonality among the statements.

2. If you use language experience materials with your students, make sure you do not begin writing the selection by having the children identify a title. Have the children identify a title *after* they have completed the writing of their language experience selection. Tell them that most authors never try to think of a title for their book until the book is completed.

3. When you are helping children read content area materials, have them notice the side headings. Lead the children to notice that usually the side headings state the main idea of the following paragraphs. Have the children find a particular side heading and read the paragraphs under it to see if the paragraphs are related to the side heading.

## ACTIVITY SHEET DIRECTIONS
### How Are We Alike? (page 9)

Use the Lesson Activity Sheet as directed during the reading lesson. In the first row, the children are looking at individual words to find out how they are alike. In the second and third rows, the children are examining or providing sentences and indicating commonality among the details.

### I Have the Main Idea — In My Hand! (page 10)

Ask the children to read the story on the Practice Activity Sheet. Then ask the children to trace one of their hands on the Activity Sheet. Instruct them to write one detail from the story on each of the fingers, then to look at the details to see how they are alike. They should then write the main idea of the story on the palm.

# How Are We Alike?

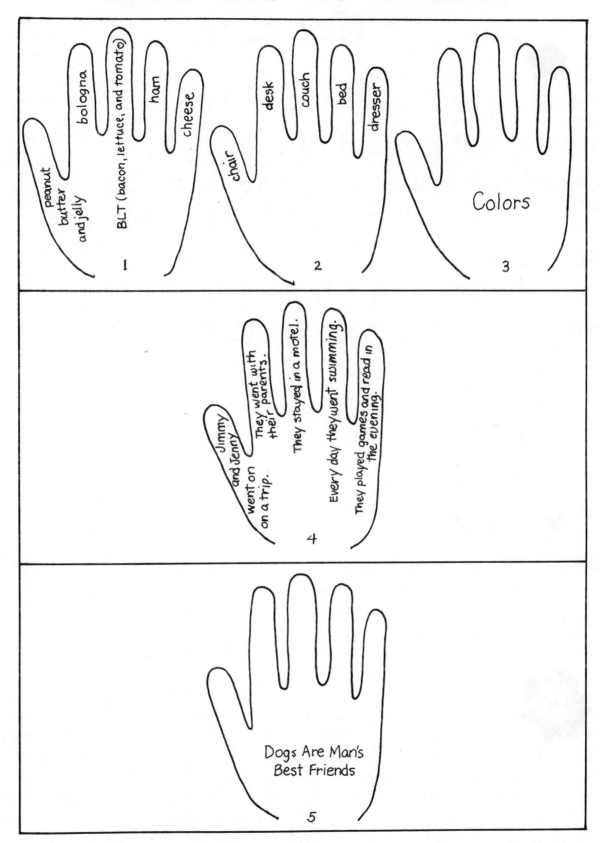

peanut butter and jelly
bologna
BLT (bacon, lettuce, and tomato)
ham
cheese

1

chair
desk
couch
bed
dresser

2

Colors

3

Jimmy and Jenny
went on on a trip.
They went with their parents.
They stayed in a motel.
Every day they went swimming.
They played games and read in the evening.

4

Dogs Are Man's Best Friends

5

From *A Reading Skillbuilder: Comprehension* © 1982 by Scott, Foresman & Co. Harry W. Forgan and Bonnie F. Striebel

# I Have the Main Idea — In My Hand!

I have a pet hamster.
One night it got out of the cage.
I could not find it for three days.
I finally found it sleeping in one of my old shoes.
It was happy to get back into the cage.
The first thing it did was to drink lots and lots of water.

From *A Reading Skillbuilder: Comprehension* © 1982 by Scott, Foresman & Co. Harry W. Forgan and Bonnie F. Striebel

# Stick to the Topic

From *A Reading Skillbuilder: Comprehension* © 1982 by Scott, Foresman & Co.
Harry W. Forgan and Bonnie F. Striebel

Dear Parents,

My teacher is teaching me how to find the main idea. The main idea tells about all the facts or details in the story. My teacher says I can make a booklet with one main idea. I can make a booklet all about foods that I like. We can call it "Foods I Like." Listed below are titles of other booklets I can make, but for each topic I must have a separate book. Could we get four or five pieces of paper and staple the pages together? If we have some old magazines, I can cut out pictures for my booklets. I will write the title on the front of the booklet and paste the pictures inside. Let me decide which topic I want to do first.

1. Foods I Like to Eat
2. My Wish Book
3. Cars I Like to See
4. My Favorite Toys
5. Things I Like to Do
6. People I Like
7. Things I Don't Like

When I am all done with my booklet I am supposed to bring it to school. I am going to show it to the other children in my class. They will have to guess what the title of my booklet is without seeing the title page.

When I am reading to you, I can tell you what the main idea of a paragraph is. I will just look at all the sentences and see how they are alike. Then I can think of a good title for the paragraph. Could I read a paragraph to you sometime and tell you what the main idea is? Thank you.

# Sequence of Events

**SPECIFIC OBJECTIVE**

The children will be able to read short selections and note the sequence in which the events take place.

**INSTRUCTIONAL READING LEVEL**

3/1–3/2. You may have some students who are reading above the third grade instructional level who still have difficulty in identifying the sequence of events. Feel free to adapt the suggestions in this lesson plan by using higher level instructional materials.

**MATERIALS**

1. The "My Birthday Wish" Lesson Activity Sheet
2. The "My Trip to Disney World" Practice Activity Sheet
3. The "I Know How Old You Are and How Much Money You Have!" Home Activity Sheet

**INSTRUCTIONAL PROCEDURES**

1. Begin this lesson by telling the children to pretend that today is their birthday. Tell the children you would like them to plan a very special birthday doing anything they would like to do. You can remind the children that there are no problems about their wishes; they will have enough money, all the people they want to be with are available, and so forth. Now give the children a copy of the "My Birthday Wish" Lesson Activity Sheet. Read the selection with the children and tell them you would like them to fill in the blanks after they have dreamed about what their favorite birthday would be like. Provide an opportunity for the children to complete the blanks.

2. After the children have finished their birthday wish papers, have them share their papers with each other. Enjoy the children as you hear about their favorite wishes.

3. Tell the children that when they are reading they should pay attention to the order in which things take place in a story. Have them look at their birthday wish papers and notice the order of the events in the day. Have them point out what time they are to get up, what they are going to do first, what they are going to do after breakfast, what they would want to do after lunch, how long they are to stay up, and so forth. Read one of the stories, reversing the order by reading about suppertime first, the time they are eating breakfast second, and so forth. Help the children to see that when the events of the story are in order, it is easier to understand. Summarize the lesson by telling the children that as they are reading, they should be paying attention to the sequence of events in a story. Tell them that authors try to put the events in order, or sequence, so it is easier for readers to understand.

**PRACTICE**

1. Provide the children with a copy of the Practice Activity Sheet and tell them that Jimmy's birthday wish was to go to Disney World. His wish came true! Have the children read the paragraph describing what Jimmy did at Disney World. Next have the children draw lines on the map of Disney World to indicate the attractions Jimmy visited — and the order in which he visited them. When the children have completed this activity, have them bring their Practice Activity Sheets to the reading circle. You may want to provide opportunities for them to share the order in which they would like to see the various attractions at Disney World.

2. Tell the children you have a magic trick for them to play on their parents. After you teach them how to do this trick, they will be able to tell how old a person is and know how much change the person has in his pocket. Go through the directions on the Home Activity Sheet and show the children what to do. Tell the children that the only thing

they have to do after they tell an adult to do the seven steps is to add 115 to the total the adult gave them. After the children have added 115 to the total, if the number is a four-digit number, the first two numbers tell how old the person is and the last two numbers tell the amount of spare change he or she has. If the children do this on a friend who is 9 years old or younger, they will get a three-digit number. In this case the first number tells the age of the friend and the other numbers tell the amount of spare change. Remind the children that this trick will not work unless they follow the sequence of events by giving the directions in order. Again, remind the children that whenever they are reading, they should pay particular attention to the sequence.

**TIPS FOR TEACHING RELATED LESSONS**

1. You can help the children notice the sequence of events by paying attention to temporal (time) words or words that indicate when something is happening. Use the following list of words to help children become aware of the temporal words as they read. Ask the children to find some of these words in their reading selections and indicate how these words help them to know when certain events are taking place in the sequence of the events.

| | |
|---|---|
| first | beginning |
| next | when |
| concluded | finally |
| while | then |
| at which time | whereupon |
| over | until |
| at that point | quickly |
| temporarily | shortly |
| forever | suddenly |
| immediately | at once |
| right away | abruptly |
| subsequently | later |
| afterwards | since |
| preceding | wherefore |
| back when | formerly |
| to date | presently |
| in due time | as of yet |
| sometime | eventually |
| about to | sooner |
| lately | thereto |
| promptly | traditionally |
| the break of day | right away |
| this afternoon | occasionally |
| constantly | now and then |
| hourly | weekly |
| momentarily | monthly |

| | |
|---|---|
| daily | intermittently |
| eventually | hurriedly |
| following | after |
| before | as |
| half-way | lastly |
| eventually | at that time |
| upon which | during |
| whenever | in the middle of |
| meanwhile | up to that time |
| slowly | at that moment |
| always | at another time |
| instantly | in a short time |
| now | without delay |
| following | consecutively |
| after | thereupon |
| thereafter | here and after |
| whereto | in the past |
| earlier | from time immemorial |
| until now | and nowadays |
| hereafter | in the long run |
| ultimately | on the point of |
| recently | on the brink or on the |
| high time | verge of |
| postpone | a short time ago |
| twilight time | in the nick of time |
| this evening | at the crack of dawn |
| rarely | this morning |
| periodically | very often |
| biweekly | once in awhile |
| annually | regularly |
| ultimately | finally |

2. Oftentimes it is valuable to have children make a list of events or directions in a particular selection. This is especially true when children are doing science experiments, when reading historical materials in social studies, or when children are reading the directions for completing a project. You can sometimes divide the children into groups and have them make a list of the sequence of important events or directions.

**ACTIVITY SHEET DIRECTIONS**
**My Birthday Wish (page 14)**

Give the children copies of the Lesson Activity Sheet and tell them to pretend that it is their birthday. Ask the children to dream about what their favorite birthday would be like. Have them fill in the blanks to describe the favorite birthday. Follow the detailed procedures in the lesson plan.

**My Trip to Disney World (page 15)**

Review the directions on the Practice Activity Sheet with the students.

# My Birthday Wish

On my next birthday I will be ____ years old. I am going to get up at ____ o'clock. The first thing I'm going to do is _____.

For breakfast I am going to eat _____.

After breakfast, I am going to _____. When I get there I'll _____.

When lunchtime comes, I am going to eat _____. Next I want to go to _____. I want to go with _____.

When it is suppertime I want _____ to be there. For supper we will have _____. After eating supper we will all _____.

When I get to open my birthday presents, I am going to open the _____ one first. It will be _____.

I want to stay up until ____ o'clock. This birthday will be one that I will never forget!

From *A Reading Skillbuilder: Comprehension* © 1982 by Scott, Foresman & Co.
Harry W. Forgan and Bonnie F. Striebel

NAME_____DATE_____

# My Trip to Disney World

**Directions:** Jimmy wanted to go to Disney World on his birthday. The story below tells about what he did when he got there. Read the paragraphs and then use a pencil to trace Jimmy's route in Disney World. Put your pencil on Start by the monorail and draw a line to show the order in which Jimmy went to his favorite places. After you complete the exercise, write a paragraph telling about what you would like to see first if you went to Disney World. Give your paragraph to another person to read and then have him or her use a different color to trace your route on the map.

From *A Reading Skillbuilder: Comprehension* © 1982 by Scott, Foresman & Co. Harry W. Forgan and Bonnie F. Striebel

Jimmy was so excited. One of his dreams was about to come true. He was going to get to go to Disney World!

After his mother had parked the car, they went to the Monorail Station to go into the main park. When they got off the monorail, Jimmy went through the gate and got his first look at Main Street. He had a hard time looking at the stores on the street because he was looking straight ahead at Cinderella's Castle.

When Jimmy and his mother got to the castle, they had to decide what they were going to do first. Jimmy had always heard about the scary ride on Space Mountain so he wanted to go there first.

After having a thrilling ride on Space Mountain, Jimmy and his mother ran to the Grand Prix Racetrack. There they waited in line for ten minutes. The wait was worth it because Jimmy got to drive his own race car around the racetrack.

After having fun on the racetrack, they decided to go to the Pirates of the Caribbean. This was one of Jimmy's favorites because he felt he was right in there with the pirates.

The next place they went to was a scary one — the Haunted House. Jimmy got to see ghosts! It even looked like a ghost was riding in his car.

Jimmy decided to go on Twenty Thousand Leagues Under the Sea next. Jimmy and his mother got to see many beautiful sea creatures.

Then they walked through the castle and went to the stores on Main Street. Jimmy was happy because he got a T-shirt with his favorite character — Mickey Mouse — on it.

Finally, Jimmy and his mother got on the monorail to go to their car.

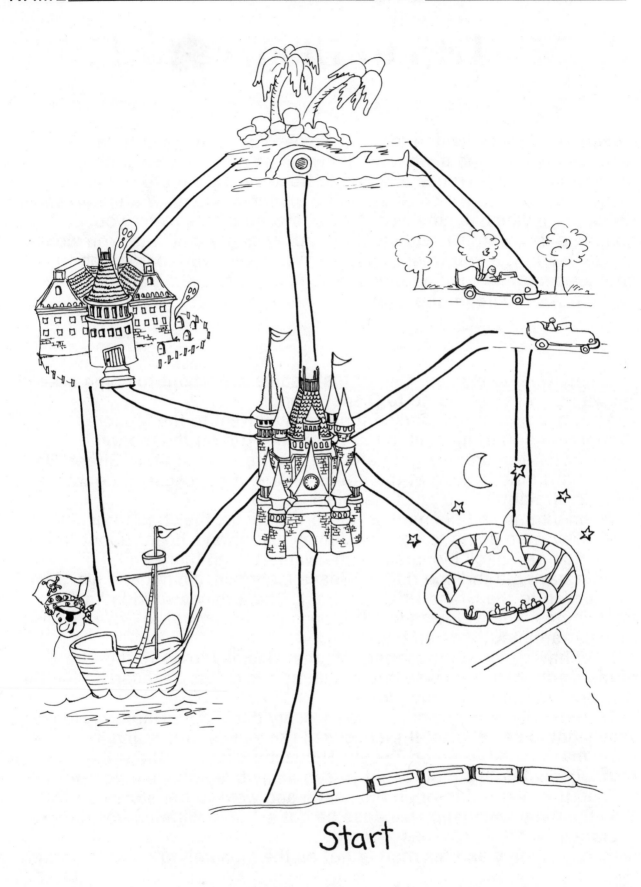

Start

# I Know How Old You Are and How Much Money You Have

From *A Reading Skillbuilder: Comprehension* © 1982 by Scott, Foresman & Co.
Harry W. Forgan and Bonnie F. Striebel

Dear Parents,

My teacher is teaching me to notice sequence of events when I read. He says it is important to know the order in which some things happen. This will help me to understand as I read. My teacher gave me a magic trick to try out on you. If I follow the sequence correctly, I will be able to find out how old people are and how much spare change they have. Let me try it out on you.

You will need to use a piece of paper and a pencil and I will tell you what to do.

1. Write down your age so I cannot see it.
2. Multiply your age by 2.
3. Add 5 to the total.
4. Multiply that number by 50.
5. Subtract 365 from that number.
6. Add your spare change under $1.00 to your number.
7. Tell me your total.

I will be able to tell you how old you are and how much spare change you have when I add 115 to your total.

You didn't know that I was a magician did you? Would you take me to the library to get some books with other magic tricks? This will help me have fun and at the same time I will be learning to read carefully so I know the order in which certain events take place. Thanks.

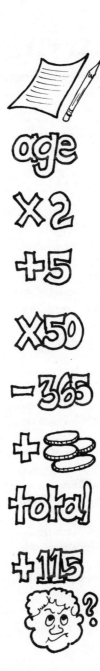

# Drawing Conclusions

## SPECIFIC OBJECTIVE

The children will be able to draw conclusions as they read and thus be able to answer questions concerning why certain events take place.

## INSTRUCTIONAL READING LEVEL

Fourth grade. This lesson presupposes that the children are able to identify details because it is necessary to locate two or more verifiable facts and use these facts to make a decision or to draw a conclusion. The materials on the Lesson Activity Sheet and the Practice Activity Sheet are written at the fourth grade reading level. You may have some students who are reading above the fourth grade level but who are still having difficulty drawing conclusions. If so, you can adapt the instructional procedures in this lesson plan.

## MATERIALS

1. The "A New Puppy" Lesson Activity Sheet
2. The "Every Dog Has His Day" Practice Activity Sheet
3. The "Ask Me Why!" Home Activity Sheet

## INSTRUCTIONAL PROCEDURES

1. Begin this lesson by telling the children that when they are reading something you expect them to draw conclusions. Ask the children what it means to draw conclusions. List the children's responses on the board and lead them to realize that when they draw conclusions they are really making decisions by thinking. When drawing conclusions, they must be able to find the facts that are available, add others if necessary, and make a summary statement or decision. Perhaps the children will want to explain drawing conclusions by simply saying that when you draw conclusions you tell why.

2. Give each child a copy of the "A New Puppy" Lesson Activity Sheet. Tell the children you would like them to read this selection to find out about the new puppy that the McDermotts got. As they read the selection, tell them to think about the following questions:

    a. Why did the McDermotts want to get a new puppy?

    b. How did the McDermott's old dog, Disney, react to the new puppy?

3. After the children have had an opportunity to read the selection, ask them why the McDermotts wanted a new puppy. Have one child read the sentences in the first paragraph, which would lead a reader to believe that the McDermotts wanted a new puppy because they wanted a dog who liked to play. Help the children to realize that when they draw conclusions or make decisions, they first must find the facts that are given. In this first paragraph the children find out that the McDermotts wanted a new puppy because Disney, their old dog, liked to sleep all the time. He never wanted to run and play with the children. Evidently the McDermotts decided to get a new puppy because they believed a new puppy would be more lively than their older dog. You can continue to ask the children some other reasons why the McDermotts might want a new puppy. Perhaps a child will say that Disney was sleeping all the time because he was lonely and needed a playmate. Maybe Disney did not want to run with the children or chase the ball because he was feeling depressed all the time. Help the children to realize that when they draw conclusions, sometimes they must add other facts that are not given in the story. If so, they are really making an inference that is based on the facts given plus the facts that the reader applies.

4. Now ask the children how Disney felt when they brought Holly home. Again, ask a child to read the facts that lead him or her to the conclusion. Perhaps the children will point out that Disney felt badly and thus he ignored the new puppy. Another child may suggest that Disney was not feeling well

and this is why he did not want to play with the puppy or eat. Help the children realize that when conclusions are drawn or when inferences are made, there may be more than one explanation.

5. Now ask the children why Disney began to play with Holly. Have them read the facts to point out that after a month, Disney and Holly began to play tag and hide-and-go-seek together. After these facts have been read or listed on the board, ask the children why they think Disney changed his behavior. Perhaps a child will suggest that Disney was feeling healthy again and ready to play. Another child may say that Disney decided it might be fun to play, so he tried it and liked it. Another child may suggest that Disney was not lonely or depressed anymore.

Continue to probe to get as many reasons as possible. Then ask the children which conclusion they feel is the best one based on the facts given in the story. Again lead the children to believe that sometimes all the facts are not provided. Feelings are not always told in the story, but as we read we must think about why certain things are happening.

6. There are other items that you can ask about the selection to encourage the children to draw conclusions. For example, you may want to ask the following questions:
   a. Why did Disney get under the bed or chair when Holly wanted to play? (Holly couldn't get to him.)
   b. Why did Holly do most of the running when the two dogs played games? (Disney was older and thus did not have as much energy.)
   c. Why did Disney have a better appetite? (He got more exercise and thus had more of a need to eat, or he accepted Holly and did not feel as badly.)
   d. Why did Disney get up bright and early every day? (It could be just to play with a puppy or to eat, but it may be that he wanted to make sure that he got attention rather than just having the new puppy get all of the attention.)

7. Conclude the lesson by reminding the children that as they are reading, you want them to be thinking about why certain things are taking place. Tell the children you will be asking them many *why* questions about the selections they will be reading.

## PRACTICE

1. Tell the children that you have a continuation of the story about the McDermott's dogs. Give each child a copy of the "Every Dog Has His Day" Practice Activity Sheet, and tell the children to read this to find out what the title means. As the children read the story, encourage them to determine why certain things happened.

2. Parents can help children draw conclusions while watching television, or by asking questions while riding in a car. The Home Activity Sheet is a letter that is designed to encourage parents to ask questions that will require the students to draw conclusions. Give the children a copy of the letter and ask them to take it home for their parents. Explain to the children that their parents may be asking them some "why" questions and, if they are not sure of the answers, to try to give a reason. Tell the children that many of the questions their parents will be asking have more than one answer, so the children should say what they believe and listen to other possible answers that might be suggested by their parents.

## TIPS FOR TEACHING RELATED LESSONS

1. As you teach additional lessons to help children draw conclusions, you may want to help them identify some key words that may give them some indication as to what conclusion to draw. These key words also help the children understand why certain things are happening in a story. Listed below are some words that you will want to have children look for as they are thinking about why certain things are happening:

| | |
|---|---|
| because | due to |
| on account of | by reason of |
| in that | so |
| therefore | since |
| seeing that | thanks to |
| for | as a result of |
| because of this | |

2. Reading materials such as the *Encyclopedia Brown* stories by Donald Sobol provide excellent opportunities for children to draw conclusions as to why certain things are happening. In the *Encyclopedia Brown* stories, children have to be detectives as they try to figure out the answers to cases. In solving the problems, children must put different facts together and draw a conclusion.

3. In addition to using reading materials to teach children to draw conclusions, I would encourage you to continue to ask children many thought-provoking questions throughout the school day. For example, you may ask the children:
   a. Why do we have traffic lights?
   b. Why do stores have sales?
   c. Why do some people have pets?
   d. Why do some people prefer cats to dogs?

e. Why do some people like to live in houses that have big yards, whereas others do not want to have their own yard?
f. Why do you have a moment of silence before the school day begins?
g. Why do some children carry their lunches while others buy their lunches at school?

## ACTIVITY SHEET DIRECTIONS
### A New Puppy (page 21)
Follow the detailed instructional procedures in the lesson plan to help children draw conclusions.

### Every Dog Has His Day (page 23)
Ask the children to read the story and answer the questions at the end.

# A New Puppy

The McDermotts got a new seven-week-old puppy yesterday. They already had one dog, Disney, but he was ten years old. Disney liked to sleep all the time and never wanted to run and play with the children. Once in awhile he would chase a ball, but usually he would just sleep.

The McDermott children decided to call their new puppy Holly. When they brought Holly home, Disney ignored her. Holly wanted to play with Disney. She tried to jump on Disney, but the old dog would just get up and walk away. Disney would usually try to get under a chair or the bed. Sometimes he did not even come out to eat.

After a month, Disney began to accept the new puppy. At times, Holly and Disney even played together. Their favorite game was tag. Holly did most of the running, while Disney stood in one spot. When Holly raced around the house and passed Disney, he would try to tag her. The two dogs liked to play hide-and-seek, too. Holly would hide and Disney would try to find her.

After six weeks the McDermotts noticed a big change in Disney. He even wanted to play with the children! When someone got a ball, both Holly and Disney wanted to chase it. Disney began to eat more and got up bright and early each day.

From *A Reading Skillbuilder: Comprehension* © 1982 by Scott, Foresman & Co. Harry W. Forgan and Bonnie F. Striebel

# Every Dog Has His Day

Disney, the ten year old dog, liked to play with his new sister, Holly, for awhile. But soon things began to change. Disney began to ignore the new puppy again. When Holly wanted to play tag, Disney would go and lie down under the bed.

Soon it was summertime and the McDermotts wanted to go on a vacation. They did not feel comfortable about leaving their dogs in a kennel. Mrs. McDermott was worried about Disney because he would not eat very much. The McDermotts found a cabin in the mountains that would accept pets. They decided to take the dogs with them. The McDermott children were especially happy that the dogs were going.

Staying in the mountains was fun. Every day the McDermotts went hiking. One day both dogs went with them. As the family hiked up the mountain, the dogs led the way. The children were picking wild flowers and raspberries. The peaceful hike was interrupted when Holly began to bark and bark. She was far ahead of the McDermott family, so no one could really tell why she was barking.

Disney ran as fast as he could to find out why Holly was barking. Just as he got to Holly, he saw a big snake ready to strike at her. Disney ran and picked up Holly by the nape of the neck. He carried her away from the snake.

The McDermotts were so thankful. They petted Disney and praised him for the good deed. Soon Disney began to play with Holly. He seemed to love the attention he was getting again!

From *A Reading Skillbuilder: Comprehension* © 1982 by Scott, Foresman & Co. Harry W. Forgan and Bonnie F. Striebel

NAME_____DATE_____

**Directions:** After you have read the story answer these questions.

1. Why did Disney begin to ignore Holly? _____

_____

2. Why didn't Mrs. McDermott want to leave the dogs in a

   kennel? _____

_____

3. Why were the children happy to take the dogs along? __

_____

4. Why did the McDermotts pet and praise Disney? _____

_____

5. How do you think Holly felt about Disney after he saved

   her? _____

_____

6. Why did Disney begin to eat again? _____

_____

7. Why is the story called, "Every Dog Has His Day?" ____

_____

From *A Reading Skillbuilder: Comprehension* © 1982 by Scott, Foresman & Co. Harry W. Forgan and Bonnie F. Striebel

PRACTICE ACTIVITY SHEET

# Ask Me Why!

Dear Parents,

My teacher is teaching me the importance of drawing conclusions while I am reading. She says that if I can understand why things are happening, I will be a better reader. She has been asking us lots of "why" questions in school.

You can help me become a better thinker and reader by asking me lots of questions about why certain things happen. When we go for rides in the car, you can ask me why there are certain traffic signs along the road. As we watch television, you can ask me why certain things are happening on the program. I always like to ask you "why" questions, and I hope you will take time to answer them for me. I am trying to figure out the reasons for things.

During the next few weeks, would you try to ask me a lot of "why" questions? I will not always know the answers, but I can try to answer your questions. Maybe you have a better answer than I do, and if you do, please tell me. Don't get angry with me if I don't know the answers to the questions, because I want to learn "why." As we read stories together, I'll try to tell you why certain things are happening. Meanwhile, when we watch television, go for walks, or ride in the car, try to ask me a lot of "why" questions.

From *A Reading Skillbuilder: Comprehension* © 1982 by Scott, Foresman & Co.
Harry W. Forgan and Bonnie F. Striebel

# Evaluating Critically

## SPECIFIC OBJECTIVE

The children will be able to distinguish facts from opinions found in written advertisements.

## INSTRUCTIONAL READING LEVEL

Fifth grade.

## MATERIALS

1. The "Is That Really True?" Lesson Activity Sheet
2. The "Buyer Beware!" Practice Activity Sheet
3. The "Don't Believe Everything You Read!" Home Activity Sheet

## INSTRUCTIONAL PROCEDURES

1. Begin this lesson by talking with the children about whether or not they believe everything they hear. Specifically, ask them if they believe everything their friends tell them or everything they hear on television. Have them point out some things they believe and some things they do not believe. If the children have difficulty thinking of examples, have them consider the following comments that might be made by their friends:
   a. The best football team is the Cleveland Browns.
   b. You need a haircut.
   c. Our teacher is the best one in the school.
   d. The earth is round.
   e. On July 4th we celebrate the independence of our country.
   f. My dad is better than your dad.
   g. It is fun to be in Scouts.
   h. The best program on TV is "Mork and Mindy."
   i. The words in the dictionary are in alphabetical order.

Have the children realize that some of the statements their friends make and some of those mentioned above are facts and others are opinions.

Point out the difference between a fact and an opinion by saying that a fact is something that can be proven to be true. An opinion is a belief that is not based on absolute certainty or positive knowledge, but rather on what one thinks to be true. Conclude this part of the lesson by helping the children realize that they should not believe everything they hear because some things are only opinions that have not been proven to be true.

2. Tell the children that when they read, they should not believe everything they see. Help the children realize that some young children believe that as long as something is in print, it is true. Tell them that this is not the case, because many times opinions are used rather than facts. Remind the children that an opinion is something someone believes that has not been proven to be true. Tell the children that many times when they see advertisements or food labels they will find some facts, but there will also be some opinions. Give the children a copy of the "Is That Really True?" Lesson Activity Sheet. Tell the children that these advertisements are similar to some they see in their magazines, but none of the advertisements are real. Tell them: "We are going to look at the advertisements to find which statements are facts that have been proven and which statements are opinions." Direct the children's attention to the first box that reads as follows:

This is a bargain! A fantastic collection of stamps from over 25 countries. All the stamps are unusual. You will get 135 stamps in all. The first 100 requests receive a bonus gift. Send 20¢ to Beautiful Stamps, 4500 NW 2nd Street, Lake Black, Ohio 44240

Go through the advertisement sentence by sentence and help the children identify which sentences are factual and which ones are opinions. Point out the facts are (1) the stamps are from over

25 countries, (2) you will get 135 stamps, (3) the first 100 people to request them will get a bonus gift that may or may not be worth something, and (4) you must send 20¢ to the address. Likewise, have the children point out that it is the advertisers opinion that (1) this is a bargain, (2) it is a fantastic collection, and (3) all the stamps are unusual. Have the children underline the facts and circle the opinions in the ad. Help them realize that advertisers try to share positive opinions about their products to get others to buy.

3. Tell the children that many of the products they buy also have opinions on the packages to try to get people to buy them. Direct the children's attention to the cereal box found on the second half of the Lesson Activity Sheet. Ask the children to read the box and again circle the opinions. (Help them realize that statements such as, "Get a great start every morning," are opinions.) The facts tell that the cereal contains eight vitamins, that there is a mirror inside that may or may not be worth anything, the weight, and the ingredients. Direct the children's attention to the coupon that shows them how advertisers try to get people to buy by making an offer in addition to the cereal. Help them circle the opinion statements pointing out words such as *great*, *whole*, and *favorite*. Then have the children underline the facts indicating the four posters, the cost, the size, the number of colors, and the address.

4. Conclude this part of the lesson by telling the children that they can't believe everything on the box because some of the statements are opinions rather than facts. Help the children realize that opinions are not necessarily lies, but rather simply what someone believes. Tell them that when they try a product or order something they have found in an advertisement, they may hold the same opinion. For example, the children may think the posters are great and that the stamps are unusual. Summarize the lesson by telling the children that buyers are told to beware. Beware means to be on the lookout for facts and statements that are simply opinions.

5. You can see how the children are coming along distinguishing the difference between facts and opinions by asking them to listen to the following statements you read and telling you whether they are facts or opinions. Use these statements:

a. You will love this flavor!
b. Money-back guarantee
c. Send 10¢
d. Hours of fun!
e. Truly the world's most unusual
f. Over 25,000 sold

g. No rip-offs
h. Here is an easy way to earn money
i. Battery operated
j. Revolutionary new design
k. Avoid disappointment — order today
l. It has a red handle

6. Conclude the lesson by telling the children to look for facts to determine whether or not they should buy something. They can also read the opinions and must determine how much faith they have in the opinions expressed in the advertisement. The important point is for them to not believe everything they read. Perhaps some of the children will describe things they have sent away for or bought, and later found out they wasted money. Tell the children they will be less likely to be "gyped" if they look for the facts first.

**PRACTICE**

1. Distribute the "Buyer Beware!" Practice Activity Sheet. Tell the children that you have some advertisements that are not real advertisements, but that are very similar to those they will find in their magazines. Direct the children to practice finding facts and opinions by reading these advertments. When they read a sentence or a part of a sentence that is a fact, they should underline it. If they read a sentence or part of a sentence that is an opinion, they should circle those words. After the children have completed this activity, check their responses and again help them distinguish between facts and opinions.

2. Parents are natural partners in helping children learn to critically evaluate what they read. Frequently children will be reading magazines at home and will ask their parents what they think about the offer. Send home the Home Activity Sheet asking the parents to help their children locate advertisements in magazines or newspapers and distinguish the facts from opinions. When the children bring their advertisements to school, compile a bulletin board of these advertisements for others in the class to see.

**TIPS FOR TEACHING RELATED LESSONS**

1. In addition to helping children look for facts and opinions as they read, you can also help the children detect other propaganda techniques. You may want to have the children bring in other advertisements that try to influence the reader to buy something because somebody famous uses it or endorses it. You can make a nice bulletin board of

these advertisements and point out to children how many advertisers use this propaganda technique to influence people. Help the children understand that just because somebody famous likes something, it does not mean everyone will like it. Tell the children that each individual has his or her own preferences, and these may be different from those of the famous person.

2. Another propaganda technique that is frequently used to influence children is that of using words that have very pleasant connotations. List some of these words on the board and discuss how advertisers use them frequently. You might use words such as: *fabulous, terrific, unusual, new, revolutionary, super, easy, exciting, free, different, wow, bargain, famous, special, amazing, genuine, greatest on earth, incredible, discount, great, miracle, value, limited offer, official, low-price, get acquainted, extra-special,* and *rush.* Have the children cut out advertisements and circle words such as these that are used to get their attention to make them believe the product is extra special.

**ACTIVITY SHEET DIRECTIONS**
**Is That Really True? (page 30)**

Direct the children to find the facts and opinions in the advertisements. The children should circle the opinions and underline the facts as they read. Sometimes a part of a sentence might be factual and another part may be opinion. Tell the children to circle only those words that are opinions and underline those words that are facts.

**Buyer Beware! (page 31)**

Review the directions on the Practice Activity Sheet with the students.

# Is That Really True?

**Directions:** Circle those words that are opinions and underline those words that are facts.

**This is a bargain!**
A fantastic collection of stamps from over 25 countries. All of the stamps are unusual! You will get 135 stamps in all. The first 100 requests receive a bonus gift! Send 20¢ to Beautiful Stamps, 4500 NW 2nd Street, Lake Black, Ohio 44240.

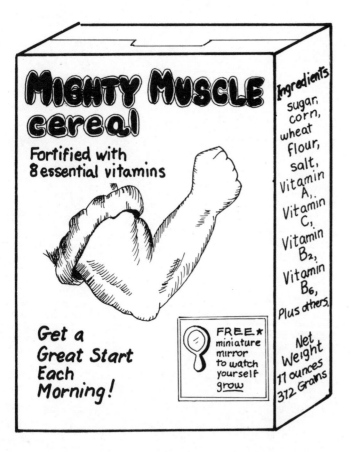

MIGHTY MUSCLE cereal

Fortified with 8 essential vitamins

Get a Great Start Each Morning!

FREE★ miniature mirror to watch yourself grow

Ingredients
sugar, corn, wheat flour, salt, Vitamin A, Vitamin C, Vitamin B₂, Vitamin B₆, Plus others.

Net Weight
11 ounces
312 Grams

**Coupon   A great offer!**
You can get 4 posters for only $1. Each poster is 12 inches by 14 inches. You can decorate your whole room. Five different colors on each poster. The posters have pictures of your favorite television stars. Send $1 plus 35¢ for handling and postage to: Posters, Box 1980, Television City, New York, New York 10017

From *A Reading Skillbuilder: Comprehension* © 1982 by Scott, Foresman & Co. Harry W. Forgan and Bonnie F. Striebel

NAME_____DATE_____

# Buyer Beware!

**Directions:** Read the four advertisements.
Underline the facts and circle the opinions. Remember, a
fact is something that is proven to be true. An opinion is
something that somebody believes to be true.

From *A Reading Skillbuilder: Comprehension* © 1982 by Scott, Foresman & Co.
Harry W. Forgan and Bonnie F. Striebel

## MAKE MONEY

You can make $500–$1,000 selling our new magazine,
*Get Smart*. Everyone who has children will want to
subscribe to *Get Smart*. This magazine has games and
educational activities that will help children get smart.
*Get Smart* sells for $2 a copy. You get to buy them from
us for $1 a copy. You make $1 every time you sell a copy.
Just fill out the coupon below to receive your first order
of 100 copies. If you sell all of them, you will earn $100. If
not, return the unsold copies and pay nothing. We think
you will sell all of them and make up to even $500 or
$1,000. This is a great opportunity! The magazines are so
easy to sell. Your friends, neighbors, and teachers will be
so happy that you are helping them get smart.

## SECRET SAFE

Now you can hide your money so no one can find it. This
safe looks like a car but on the bottom of the car there
is a combination lock. Keep all of your money inside of it
and it will be safe. The car hold $5 worth of quarters. You
can fool your friends. Send $3 to Hide-Your-Money, Box
1099, New York, New York 10017

## HYPNOTIZE YOUR FRIENDS

It is easy to hypnotize your friends. You can make people obey your commands. Ten lessons — each on a separate card. These lessons will help you strengthen your memory, too. Send 50¢ to Do-What-I-Say, Box 17, Tub, Maine 04532

## ID BRACELET!

Gold with a gold chain. Look like 24k gold. Will print anything you want on it. You get two lines with 10 letters each. Your friends will envy you. Only $2. If you want us to rush your bracelet today, send $2 to Gold Craft, Box 24, Karet, Tennessee 37401

From *A Reading Skillbuilder: Comprehension* © 1982 by Scott, Foresman & Co. Harry W. Forgan and Bonnie F. Striebel

# Don't Believe Everything You Read

Dear Parents,

My teacher is teaching me not to believe everything I read. She said this is really important when I am reading advertisements. Sometimes the advertisers include their opinions rather than the proven facts. I have been reading some advertisements to find the facts and the opinions. The teacher wants me to look at some of my magazines and newspapers to find advertisements. After I find them, I am to underline the facts and circle the opinions. Will you help me with the one below?

Grow earthworms. Make money fast raising earthworms. We'll teach you how to raise earthworms and tell you where to sell them. You can earn up to $1,000 a year. Send $1 for information on how you can start your own business.

From *A Reading Skillbuilder: Comprehension* © 1982 by Scott, Foresman & Co. Harry W. Forgan and Bonnie F. Striebel

# Vocabulary Development

## SPECIFIC OBJECTIVE

The children will be able to use the words *loiter*, *loitering*, and *loitered* in sentences to demonstrate they understand the meaning of them.

## INSTRUCTIONAL READING LEVEL

Fourth grade.

## MATERIALS

1. The "No Loitering" Lesson Activity Sheet
2. The "100 Word Club" Practice Activity Sheet
3. The "Words I Need to Read" Home Activity Sheet
4. 3 × 5 index cards

## INSTRUCTIONAL PROCEDURES

1. Begin this lesson by giving the children a copy of the "No Loitering" Lesson Activity Sheet. Direct their attention to the title at the top of the page that says, "No Loitering." Tell them to look at the pictures of the children who are loitering. Write the word *loiter* on the chalkboard, and ask the children to tell you what they think it means after they have looked at the pictures. If they have not heard of the word, explain that *loiter* means to waste time. Clarify further by saying that when you loiter, you are just standing around doing nothing. Have the children say the word. You may want to point out the fact that the word has two syllables and the first syllable has the diphthong /oi/. Talk with the children about the pictures and have them explain why loitering is not allowed on a bridge, in front of a store, or outside of class during school hours. Ask the children if they have seen the word *loiter* in any other place.

2. Divide the children into three groups and ask members of each group to dramatize a scene in which the children are loitering. After the group members dramatize the scene, have the children use the words *loiter*, *loitering*, or *loitered* in sentences to describe the scene.

3. Tell the children you are going to give them some sentences and you want them to tell you what the sentences mean. Use the following:
   a. The clerk asked the children to leave because they were *loitering* in front of his store.
   b. He saw the accident while he was *loitering* on the bridge.
   c. She *loitered* on her way to school.
   d. We worked hard all day. We did not have time to *loiter*.

4. Ask the children if they can think of any other words that mean almost the same as *loitering*. See if they mention *linger*, *dillydally*, *being idle*, or *wasting time*. Now have the children see if they can supply words that mean the opposite of *loitering*. Help them realize that the opposite of *loitering* means being very busy or doing something.

5. Now provide each child in the group with a 3 × 5 card. Have them write the word *loitering* on one side of the card. On the other side of the card have them write, "Loitering means to waste time." Now have the children write sentences using the words *loiter*, *loitering*, and *loitered*. Tell the children that you would like to have them keep a record of new words they are learning by making a 3 × 5 card for every word. On each card they should write the word on one side in large letters. The back of the card should be used to write the definition of the word and the sentences illustrating the use of the word. Advise the children to make cards for words they learn while reading their textbooks, words they hear their parents use, or words that are used in the classroom. Tell the children that when they have 100 words they should inform you. At that time you will shuffle the 100 words, flash ten of the words to them, and see if they can read the words and use them in sentences. If they can, they become members of The 100 Word Club. Make a

chart or get a wooden plaque on which you can have the children write or woodburn their names for others to see.

## PRACTICE

1. If you were enthusiastic as you introduced "The 100 Word Club" idea to the children, they will be eager to get as many words as possible as soon as possible. Tell the children that you have another word they will sometimes see on signs. Give the children a copy of the Practice Activity Sheet that shows the 3 × 5 card with the word *potable* on it. Explain to the children that *potable* means drinkable. Have the children notice the boy taking a drink from the water fountain. Use the word potable in the sentence by saying, "The boy is drinking potable water." Ask the children if any of them have seen the word. Remember to give the children an opportunity to say the word and use it frequently during the next few days. Direct the children to make a 3 × 5 card with the word *potable* and to find other words they are learning. Use the 3 × 5 cards the children are making to help all the children increase their vocabularies.

2. Tell the children that their parents can help them learn to read and understand many words. Explain to the children that you are sending a letter home telling their parents to point out words they see when they go places together. You may want to help the children realize how many words they see on doors by directing their attention to the picture. Tell the children that when they are with their parents and they see words they cannot read, they should ask their parents what these words are and what they mean.

## TIPS FOR TEACHING RELATED LESSONS

1. Perhaps you noticed that in the lesson plan for teaching the word *loitering*, many different techniques were used to explain the meaning of the word. First, pictures were used to help the children realize what the word loitering means. Second, the children demonstrated their understanding of the word by using it in sentences. Third, the children identified the meaning of the word in sentences that you provided. Fourth, you and/or the children supplied synonyms and antonyms for the word. Finally, you pointed out the sounds of the word and had the children say it.

Vocabulary development is one of the most important jobs of teachers throughout the entire school day. Make sure you take opportunities to help children increase their vocabularies, not by telling them to look up words, but rather by using

your expertise as a teacher. The more enthusiastic you are about vocabulary development, the larger the students' vocabularies will become.

2. One part of vocabulary development that is sometimes confusing to children deals with the fact that some of our words are homonyms. You will want to help the children realize that some words have different meanings even though they sound alike. The following are some commonly used homonyms that you will want children to understand:

| | |
|---|---|
| bear - bare | wait - weight |
| hare - hair | here - hear |
| not - knot | to - too - two |
| read - reed | but - butt |
| bow - bough | maid - made |
| tail - tale | pane - pain |
| dye - die | piece - peace |
| steal - steel | whole - hole |
| new - knew | wring - ring |
| write - right | so - sew |
| by - buy | weak - week |
| sale - sail | no - know |
| cents - sense | you're - your |
| rains - reigns | see - sea |
| I - eye - aye | pier - peer |
| miner - minor | son - sun |
| for - four | there - their |
| night - knight | male - mail |
| flea - flee | brakes - breaks |
| beets - beats | rote - wrote |
| tied - tyed | waste - waist |
| wood - would | capital - capitol |
| aloud - allowed | our - hour |
| flour - flower | tee - tea |
| lay - lei | wrap - rap |
| him - hymn | loan - lone |
| heard - herd | board - bored |
| fourth - forth | need - kneed |
| bury - berry | steak - stake |
| doe - dough | Mary - merry - marry |
| ant - aunt | stationery - stationary |
| some - sum | pray - prey |
| red - read | road - rode |
| weigh - way | through - threw |
| week - weak | tail - tale |
| passed - past | seamed - seemed |
| we - wee | meat - meet |

3. Another part of the vocabulary development as far as the English language is concerned is the fact that we have so many cliches, or familiar expressions, that are sometimes unfamiliar to children. Frequently children will take the literal inter-

pretation of these cliches and thus not understand what they are reading. Take time to explain the meanings of the following cliches and familiar expressions that sometimes appear in elementary school reading material.

It takes two to tango
Cute as a button
Shape up or ship out
Neat as a pin
Everything is shipshape
Don't cry over spilled milk
So near and yet so far
Gentle as a lamb
Fit as a fiddle
What you don't know won't hurt you
Only the good die young
Never say die
Talk is cheap
Always a bridesmaid, never a bride
A penny for your thoughts
That's the way the cookie crumbles
Waste not, want not
Beauty is only skin deep
Like taking candy from a baby
A man's home is his castle
Penny wise and pound foolish
Lightning never strikes twice
We're just one big happy family
May all your troubles be little ones
Hungry as a bear
Chip off the old block
That's the way the ball bounces
Love is blind
Too many cooks spoil the broth
High as a kite
That's a horse of a different color
The sky is the limit
Haste makes waste
All that glitters is not gold
Contented as a cow
The show must go on
You can't take it with you
Live a little
From rags to riches
He works like a horse
A meal fit for a king
She is as good as gold
Sharp as a tack
Snug as a bug in a rug
Purr like a kitten
A penny saved is a penny earned
Seeing is believing
Clean as a whistle

Wise as an owl
Crazy as a fox
Don't be a stick in the mud
I should have stayed in bed
Half a loaf is better than none
It's always darkest before the dawn
Money talks
Monkey see, monkey do
It shouldn't happen to a dog
Ignorance is bliss
No rest for the weary
Easy come, easy go
You only live once
Solid as the Rock of Gibraltar
A lick and a promise

## ACTIVITY SHEET DIRECTIONS
### No Loitering (page 37)
Use the Lesson Activity Sheet to help the children understand the meaning of the word *loitering*. Detailed directions are found in the instructional procedures.

### 100 Word Club (page 38)
Direct the children to make a 3 × 5 card for each new word they learn. Begin by helping them make a 3 × 5 card for the word *loitering*. After the children have done so, tell them another new word that they can learn is *potable*. Explain the meaning of the word *potable* by demonstrating the fact that you are drinking *potable* water. Compare the word *potable* to the word *edible* and help the children realize that edible applies to food and potable applies to beverages. Tell the children that when something is *potable*, they can drink it. Ask the children where they might find a sign with the word *potable*. After the children understand the meaning of the word, help them make the 3 × 5 card for this new word, too. Direct the children to find other words in their textbooks and words they hear that are unfamiliar. The children should make a 3 × 5 card for each new word and let you know when they have 100 new words. Randomly select ten words from the child's pile and flash these to him. If the child knows how to read the word, can define it, and can use it in a sentence, it is correct. If the child gets all ten of the words that you randomly selected correct, he is a member of the 100 Word Club. Allow the child to write or woodburn his name on a chart or plaque to show others.

# No Loitering

# 100 Word Club

potable

From *A Reading Skillbuilder: Comprehension* © 1982 by Scott, Foresman & Co.
Harry W. Forgan and Bonnie F. Striebel

pō-tə-b´l

drinkable; a liquid
you can drink; The
water that comes
out of our faucet is
potable.

# Words I Need to Read

Dear Parents,

I am learning to read many different words that we see when we go places together. My teacher said it would be helpful if you could point out some of these words to me and tell me the meanings of them. The picture below shows some of the words that I can read or should be able to read. On the attached list are other words my teacher would like me to learn to read. When we go places together, will you point out these words and explain the meanings to me?

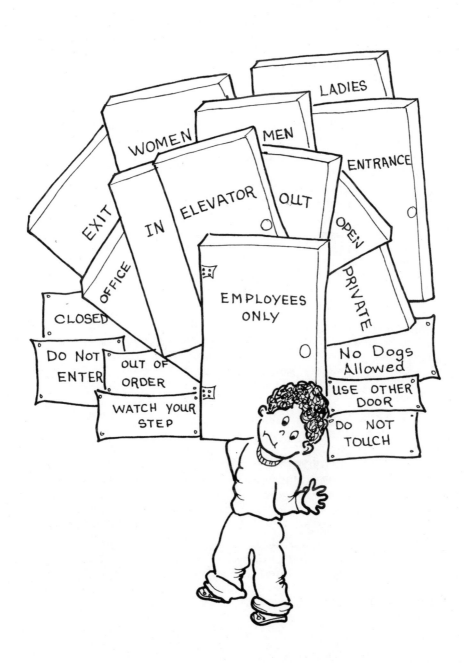

*Avoiding Accidents* Accidents are the number one cause of death of children. You can help your child avoid accidents by teaching some of the words commonly found around the house to warn children of danger. Take advantage of opportunities to point these words out to your child again and again.

| | | |
|---|---|---|
| handle with care | keep medicines out of the | kerosene |
| poison | reach of children | this end up |
| do not use near open flame | do not inhale fumes | use in open air |
| external use only | do not use near heat | fragile |
| chlorine | gasoline | combustible |
| warning | | |

*Buildings* Children and adults are required to read many signs when in public and private buildings. Again, take advantage of opportunities to point the following words out to your child so he can learn to read them as soon as possible. These words can save embarrassment and perhaps a life.

| | | |
|---|---|---|
| no dogs allowed | entrance | women |
| combustible | pull | in |
| do not touch | fallout shelter | out |
| employees only | watch step | emergency exit only |
| exit | wet paint | no minors |
| elevator | fire extinguisher | no touching |
| out of order | handle with care | office |
| ladies | information | closed |
| do not enter | fire escape | private |
| fragile | first aid | use other door |
| do not push | gentlemen | this end up |
| hands off | keep closed at all times | step down (up) |
| open | men | push |

*Be Careful* There are some words your child will encounter as he moves about your neighborhood and community that he should know for safety's sake. As you go for walks with your child or take bicycle rides, take advantage of the opportunities to point out the following words. Talk about them and help your child learn to read them as soon as possible.

| | | |
|---|---|---|
| beware | shallow water | keep off |
| deep water | don't walk | no diving |
| no swimming | warning | no fishing |
| explosives | merging traffic | keep away |
| flammable | high voltage | fallout shelter |
| keep to the left (right) | condemned | police |
| pedestrians prohibited | quiet | thin ice |
| keep out | no trespassing | 4-way stop |
| no fires | beware of dog | danger |
| no hunting | flammable | stop |
| no left (right) turn | contaminated | yield |
| out of order | | |

From *A Reading Skillbuilder: Comprehension* © 1982 by Scott, Foresman & Co. Harry W. Forgan and Bonnie F. Striebel

# Rates of Comprehension

## SPECIFIC OBJECTIVE

The children will be able to state the three reading rates and give examples of when each rate is appropriate in terms of the reader's purpose and the nature of the material.

## INSTRUCTIONAL READING LEVEL

Fourth grade or above.

## MATERIALS

1. The "Three Speeds" Lesson Activity Sheet
2. The "Watch Your Speed" Practice Activity Sheet
3. The "Your Child's Reading Rates" Home Activity Sheet

## INSTRUCTIONAL PROCEDURES

1. Begin this activity by asking the children how many speeds they have on their bicycles. Some of the children will have a one-speed bike. Others may have a three-speed, a five-speed, or a ten-speed bike. Talk with the children about why some bikes have only one speed and others have more. Review with them the fact that a three-speed bike has an advantage over a one-speed bike in that the rider can change speeds depending upon how level the ground is. Give each child a copy of the Lesson Activity Sheet and direct the children's attention to the illustration of the three different speeds. Talk about the fact that when we are peddling to get up hills, we may use the low speed, which makes it easier to pedal. When we are riding on level ground, we might use the normal or neutral speed. When we are coming down a hill, we may use the high speed. Discuss the fact that different bicycle riders use different speeds depending on what they want to do. For example, a bicycle rider might use the low speed on level ground if he just wants to ride along slowly. Another bicycle rider may use the high speed on level ground if he wants to go

faster. Summarize the discussion by telling the children that some bicycle riders prefer three speeds so that they have different choices depending on the land and the way they want to ride the bike.

2. Tell the children a good reader also has more than one speed. Explain that a good reader is like a rider of a three-speed bicycle. A good reader has three different speeds. One speed is the *slow* rate of reading. Ask the children what and when they should read slowly. Help them see that if they are following directions, studying some information, or simply reading to enjoy the author's descriptions, they may want to read slowly. Continue by saying another rate of reading good readers have is the *normal* rate of reading. Again discuss when the normal rate might be used. Help the children realize the normal rate of reading is used when reading stories for enjoyment, or information they find interesting. Finally, tell the children that good readers also have a *rapid* rate of reading and discuss when the rapid rate is useful. Help the children realize they may use a rapid rate of reading when skimming to find specific information or reading to get the central idea. Summarize this discussion by helping the children see the rate of reading depends upon (a) what is being read and (b) the reader's purpose.

3. After the children are aware of the three different rates of reading and realize they should use a different rate according to what material they are reading and their purpose in reading it, help them realize that they may read some parts of a reading assignment rapidly, other parts slowly, and other parts at a normal rate. Give an example from one of your content areas such as social studies. Help the children understand that when they are reading materials in social studies, they may want to study some of the ideas to remember them. If so, they will want to use a slow rate. If the children are reading silently to gather information that need not be

memorized, they may use a normal rate of reading. Finally, if children are reading an assignment in their social studies book to find out about the name of a particular place where a battle occurred, they may read rapidly to get to that part of the book that deals with the battle. Talk with the children about the fact that a good reader is not a fast reader, but rather a good reader is one who uses all three speeds.

4. Now direct the children's attention to the remainder of the Lesson Activity Sheet. Tell them you have different situations for reading and you want to know which speed — slow, normal, or fast the reader should use. Have the children read the descriptions and then discuss the appropriate speed.

5. When you give reading assignments, ask the children what speed they will be using before they read the assignment.

## PRACTICE

1. Tell the children you would like them to make a bulletin board or a large poster to help other students realize that good readers have three different speeds. Say you are concerned because many children believe that good readers are fast readers. For example, you may want to tell them you have noticed that sometimes when you have introduced a story or made a reading assignment, many children try to turn the page at the same time that the first child turns it, even though they may not be through reading that page. Tell the children you would like a bulletin board so other children can realize the use of the three speeds.

Give each child a copy of the "Watch Your Speed" Practice Activity Sheet, which shows different speed limits. Discuss the fact that good readers are like good drivers — they use different speeds. Tell the children you would like them to make a poster similar to this one, but you also want them to include samples of when different speeds are appropriate. For example, in the fifteen mile per hour zone, children may put a string or draw a line from the fifteen mph speed limit sign to a 3 × 5 card that shows when slow reading is important. The card might say, "When you are reading the directions to learn how to play a game, make sure you read them slowly so you know exactly what to do." For the normal rate of reading, have the children draw a line or attach a string from the 35 mph speed limit zone to an example of when a normal rate is used. The children may make a card that says, "When you are reading a good book from the library, you will probably use the normal rate of reading." Finally, tell the children to draw a line or

attach a string from the 55 mph speed limit sign to an example of when the rapid rate is being used. The children might say that "When you are looking in a telephone book for a particular name, you want to read rapidly to find the name that you are looking for." Have the children look at different types of written materials and talk about the reader's purpose in reading the materials. After the children have finished their posters or the bulletin board, have them share it with others in the class or another class.

2. Tell the children you have a letter for their parents that explains the three different rates of reading. Give the children a copy of the letter to take home to their parents. When the children are reading with their parents, encourage them to show their parents that they know when to use the various rates of reading.

## TIPS FOR TEACHING RELATED LESSONS

1. You may want to determine if the children's normal rate of reading is appropriate for their instructional reading level. To find the rate of reading, you simply have the child read a selection at his independent level for one minute. After the child has read the selection, count the number of words he has read, and this will tell you how many words he has read in a minute. According to research done at the Educational Developmental Laboratories, the typical first grade child can read 80 words per minute, the typical second grader reads 115 words per minute, the typical third grader reads 138 words per minute, the typical fourth grader reads 158 words per minute, the typical fifth grader reads 173 words per minute, and the typical sixth grader reads 185 words per minute.

The rates of reading get faster as children move through the grades because their eyes are better trained for the reading process. For example, the typical first grader makes 224 fixations, that is, a pause that lasts only a fraction of a second during which the eyes can see. By the time a child reaches sixth grade, he only makes 120 fixations per 100 words. In addition, because children's sight vocabularies increase as they progress through the grades, they do not need to make as many regressions. A regression is a movement of the eyes backwards to get a second look at something that was not clearly seen. The typical first grader makes 52 regressions in 100 words, but the typical sixth grader makes only 25 regressions in 100 words.

Another reason that rates of reading can be improved as children proceed through the grades is that children are able to increase their average span of recognition. The span of recognition deals with the amount a reader can see at one fixation. The typical first grader's span of recognition is about half a word (.45), whereas the typical sixth grader's span of recognition is .83, or almost a complete word.*

2. If you have parents who pressure you to have the children read rapidly, explain the three different rates and the fact that children's eyes simply are not ready for speed reading. Tell them that the eyes continue to develop so that the children make fewer fixations and regressions as they read. Likewise, children are able to increase their span of recognition and therefore will improve in their rate of reading during the junior high and senior high school years.

## ACTIVITY SHEET DIRECTIONS

### Three Speeds (page 45)

After introducing the lesson, have the children discuss when they should use the slow, the normal, and the rapid rates of reading for each of the paragraphs presented below. Help the children realize that the rate of reading depends not only on the type of material, but on the reader's purpose.

### Watch Your Speed (page 47)

Ask the children to read the directions on the Practice Activity Sheet. Then ask them to make their own poster or bulletin board as discussed in the detailed lesson plan.

*The information concerning eye movement norms was compiled by S.W. Taylor, H. Frackenpohl, and J. L. Pette, "Grade Level Norms for the Component of the Fundamental Reading Skill," *Research Information Bulletin*, No. 3 (Huntington, New York: Educational Developmental Laboratories, 1960), p. 12.

# Three Speeds

1. You are reading a birthday invitation you got in the mail. You want to find out who the party is for, what time it is, what day it is, and the address of the person. Would you read this information slowly, at a normal rate, or rapidly?

2. You went to the library and checked out a book that you once read and enjoyed. Because you liked the book, you want to read it again. Would you read it at a slow rate, a normal rate, or a rapid rate?

3. In your math class, you must do some written problems. For example, one problem says, "When the summer vacation was about to begin, Bobby had 124 miles on his bicycle. At the end of the summer his odometer read 278 miles. How many miles did Bobby ride his bike during the summer vacation? Should you use a slow, a normal, or a rapid rate of reading?

4. You are looking for your friend's telephone number in the directory. Would you use a slow, a normal, or a rapid rate of reading to locate your friend's name?

5. Your teacher has asked you to memorize a poem to tell your classmates. When studying the poem, should you read at a slow rate of reading, a normal rate of reading, or a rapid rate of reading?

6. You are reading an advertisement about sending away for stamps for your stamp collection. Would you read the advertisement at a slow, a normal, or a rapid rate of reading?

From *A Reading Skillbuilder: Comprehension* © 1982 by Scott, Foresman & Co. Harry W. Forgan and Bonnie F. Striebel

7. Your teacher has asked you to read pages 117 to 121 in your social studies book. She says that she is going to give you a quiz on what you have read. Would you read those pages at a slow rate of reading, a normal rate, or a rapid rate of reading?

8. You are putting together a model. Would you read the directions at a slow rate of reading, a normal rate of reading, or a rapid rate of reading?

9. You are looking to see what is on television tonight. You get the *TV Guide* and begin to look at the names of the programs. Would you read them at a slow rate of reading, a normal rate, or a rapid rate of reading?

10. You found a television program you think you want to watch. There is a description of it as well as information about what channel it is on. Would you read this at a slow, a normal, or a rapid rate of reading?

11. You are reading a story to your younger sister. You come to the part that is very sad. Would you read that at a slow rate of reading, a normal rate of reading, or a rapid rate of reading?

From *A Reading Skillbuilder: Comprehension* © 1982 by Scott, Foresman & Co. Harry W. Forgan and Bonnie F. Striebel

NAME_____ DATE_____

# Watch Your Speed

**Directions:** Look at the picture to notice the three different speed limits. Cars are expected to go 15 miles an hour when they are driving near a school. In neighborhoods, cars are limited to 35 miles an hour. On highways in the country, cars can go faster — up to 55 miles an hour.

Good readers are like good drivers. Sometimes good readers go slowly, other times at a normal rate, and at times very fast.

From *A Reading Skillbuilder: Comprehension* © 1982 by Scott, Foresman & Co.
Harry W. Forgan and Bonnie F. Striebel

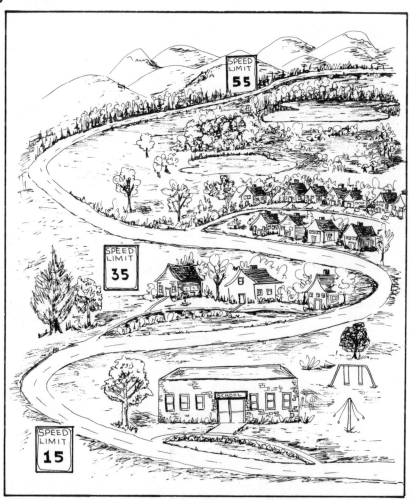

Your teacher will tell you how you can make a poster or a bulletin board to show others the three different speeds a good reader uses.

# Your Child's Reading Rates

Dear Parents,

My teacher is helping me learn the speed at which I should read different written materials. She says that there are three rates good readers use. Sometimes good readers read *slowly*. I want to use the *slow* rate of reading when I am studying information, reading the directions on how to play a game, or when I am putting a model together.

The second rate of reading is called the *normal* rate of reading. My teacher says that this is the rate I should use when I am reading my library books or stories in a magazine. The normal rate of reading is used when I want to enjoy what I am reading without trying to memorize the information.

The *rapid* rate of reading is one I should use when I am reading to find the main idea of something. I can also use the rapid rate when I am skimming material to locate particular information.

I need to learn when to use the three different rates of reading. The rate I choose depends on what I am reading and why I am reading it. For example, if I am reading a math problem that I must solve, I must read it slowly to find out what the question is and what the facts are.

A good reader is not just a fast reader. A good reader is someone who can read slowly, normally, and rapidly.

You can help me by reminding me of which rate I should use when I read different types of materials. Sometimes you will want to tell me to slow down; other times you will want to encourage me to read faster. Will you do this?

From *A Reading Skillbuilder: Comprehension* © 1982 by Scott, Foresman & Co. Harry W. Forgan and Bonnie F. Striebel.

READING GAME RULES

READING LIBRARY BOOK

READING TELEPHONE BOOK

# Oral Reading

**SPECIFIC OBJECTIVE**

The children will be able to evaluate their effectiveness when reading orally and will select and practice one oral reading skill to increase their proficiency in reading aloud to others.

**INSTRUCTIONAL READING LEVEL**

Third grade or above.

**MATERIALS**

1. The "Listen To This" Lesson Activity Sheet
2. The "Expressing Feelings" Practice Activity Sheet
3. The "Reading with Your Child" Home Activity Sheet
4. Tape recorder

**INSTRUCTIONAL PROCEDURES**

1. Begin this lesson by talking with the children about when they need to read orally. Lead them to realize that most of the reading they do is silent reading, however, there are times when they must read out loud to others. Be sure to discuss experiences such as reading parts of library books, giving oral reports, reading newspaper clippings, reading materials to someone over the telephone, reading to prove a point, reading stories to younger children, and the times during the school day when you ask the children to read orally. Summarize this part of the lesson by telling the children that because they *do* read orally to others, they must be able to do it well; otherwise the audience or listener is bored. Talk about how they feel when they listen to someone who cannot read well orally. Tell the children you can help each one of them to become an excellent oral reader so others will want to listen.

2. At this time ask the children what a good oral reader does when reading. Have them think of the person they feel is the best oral reader they have heard (teacher, parent, clergyman, peer) and ask why that person is so good. As the children suggest characteristics, list them on the board. Hopefully the children will mention that a good oral reader is someone who displays many of the following characteristics:

   a. reads with expression
   b. reads in thought units or phrases rather than word by word
   c. pays attention to punctuation marks
   d. has appropriate volume, pitch, and tone
   e. says each word clearly and distinctly
   f. reads at an appropriate rate so the audience can understand
   g. knows all the words and keeps his or her place while reading

3. Contrast the characteristics of an effective oral reader and a poor oral reader by reading the selection on the Lesson Activity Sheet in two distinctly different ways. When you read it the first time, demonstrate the many errors made by a poor oral reader. That is, read word by word, in a monotone, pausing to figure out some of the words, and ignoring some of the punctuation marks. Also, use an inappropriate rate and volume. Mumble some of the words rather than saying each one clearly. When you read it the second time demonstrate the characteristics of an effective oral reader. After having read both ways, review the characteristics of effective oral readers.

4. Tell the children that you know each one of them has some strengths as an oral reader. You may want to point out specific skills certain children demonstrate as they read orally. At the same time, tell the children that each person can also work to improve his or her oral reading. Tell the children that you are going to ask each one of them to read a paragraph into the tape recorder. After the children have done so, you will replay the tape and the children will listen carefully to evaluate each other. At

this time distribute copies of the "Listen to This" Lesson Activity Sheet. Have the children read the selection silently to make sure they know all of the words; then have each child in turn read the selection into the tape recorder.

5. Now direct the children's attention to the second half of the Lesson Activity Sheet, which includes a list of the characteristics of an effective oral reader. Tell the children that you are going to play the tape recorder and stop it after each reader. The children are to listen carefully and then point out two strengths that they noticed as the individual was reading. Also, ask the children to point out one weakness or skill that each reader needs to improve. Guide the children in noting their own strengths and any areas they want to improve.

6. Conclude this lesson by telling the children that they now have some idea of their strengths and weaknesses as an oral reader. Tell them you want each one to choose one characteristic he or she would like to work on. Have the children set one goal and then tell them to practice this skill using the tape recorder and reading the selection contained on the "Expressing Feelings" Practice Activity Sheet.

## PRACTICE

1. Introduce the "Expressing Feelings" Practice Activity Sheet by telling the children that when they read orally they are really putting on a play. As an actor or an actress, the oral reader is expected to read to express the feelings of the character or situation just as if they were involved in a play. Tell the children that you would like them to practice reading with expression and to work on the one skill that each person wants to improve. Direct the children's attention to the four selections on the Practice Activity Sheet. Ask the children to read each selection carefully and decide how the character feels. After the children are aware of the situation, they will want to think about what rate of reading and what volume and pitch they should use to express the feelings appropriately. Direct the children to take turns reading a paragraph from the Practice Activity Sheet into a tape recorder. After each child has had an opportunity to read a paragraph into the tape recorder, he or she should listen to each other to evaluate their oral reading skills. They may want to retape certain paragraphs to demonstrate improvements.

2. Send home copies of the "Reading with Your Child" Home Activity Sheet. Many parents are willing to help their child with oral reading and can be effective if they follow the guidelines in the letter.

Before sending home the letter, be sure to talk with the children about what materials they may want to read with their parents. Be certain that the children have materials at their free or independent reading level in which they recognize nearly every word and have no difficulties with comprehension.

## TIPS FOR TEACHING RELATED LESSONS

1. Listed below are sentences including different types of punctuation marks that children can use as they practice paying attention to particular types of punctuation marks. You may want to talk with the children about the punctuation marks and the implications for oral reading.

a. Periods
1. I would like to go out and play kickball today.
2. Please take that out of your mouth.
3. This is a beautiful day for staying indoors.
4. I think I'd like to have apple pie.
5. I lost my two front teeth when I was six years old.
6. My favorite month of the year is July.

b. Commas, Semicolons, Colons, and Dashes
1. There are three things that I am afraid of: snakes, bats, and chickens.
2. Yes, I would like to do that.
3. It was a long time until they came, however, when we saw them we were happy.
4. Mothers do get angry; however, sometimes they have a right to be angry.
5. I would like to do that — if you will let me.
6. Tom's favorite fruits are apples, bananas, oranges, and grapes.
7. Yes, Judy, you are able to do it.

c. Exclamation Marks
1. I said be quiet!
2. I don't want to go!
3. She surely is pretty!
4. I said get out of here!
5. You can read!
6. We won!

d. Question Marks
1. How many miles is it to your grandmother's house?
2. Where did you get that terrible looking hat?
3. Do you have any pets?
4. Why do we have to do this?
5. What is your favorite kind of ice cream?
6. Did you watch anything on TV last night?

e. Quotation Marks
1. Tom said, "I had a great summer."

2. The teacher stood there for a moment and finally spoke: "I had to wait too long!"
3. "Susie didn't do that," said Tom.
4. "I can go," said Susie, "if I want to."
5. "Why don't you just sit down and cry," said her dad.

## ACTIVITY SHEET DIRECTIONS

### Listen to This (page 53)
Review the directions on the Lesson Activity Sheet with the students.

### Expressing Feelings (page 55)
Review the directions on the Practice Activity Sheet with the students.

From *A Reading Skillbuilder: Comprehension* © 1982 by Scott, Foresman & Co. Harry W. Forgan and Bonnie F. Striebel

# Listen to This

**Directions:** Below you will find a paragraph you can read aloud into the tape recorder. Make sure you read the following story silently before you read it into the tape recorder. After you have recorded the story, the teacher will play it back. You and your classmates should listen carefully to see what you do well as an oral reader. Your teacher and your classmates should tell you one thing you could do to improve your skill as an oral reader.

## Selection to Be Read Aloud

It was summertime and Jennifer was supposed to be having fun. She was visiting her cousins at their summer cabin. When she asked her cousins to play, everyone said she was too small. Nobody invited her to play games or to go hiking. Finally Jennifer decided to go fishing. Her uncle put a worm on the hook and she sat at the edge of the boathouse and dropped the line into the water. She knew she wouldn't catch a fish — she had never caught one in her life. She sat there looking out at the still water. After a few minutes, her bobber went under water! She pulled the pole as quickly as she could. She saw the pole starting to bend and she knew she had a big one! She screamed for help and every one of her cousins came. Before they got there, however, Jennifer had a big fish — a seven-pounder — out of the water. All of the children began to treat Jennifer differently. They knew she was able to do lots of things!

When you read orally, did you:
1. Read the sentences the way the characters would have said them?
2. Read in phrases rather than word by word?
3. Pay attention to the punctuation marks?
4. Use the right volume?
5. Say each word clearly?
6. Read at the right rate?
7. Know the words and keep your place?

From *A Reading Skillbuilder: Comprehension* © 1982 by Scott, Foresman & Co. Harry W. Forgan and Bonnie F. Striebel

# Expressing Feelings

**Directions:** Listed below are four paragraphs. In each one of the paragraphs a different feeling is expressed. Read the paragraphs silently to see how the character feels. After you know how the character feels, read the paragraph into a tape recorder trying to say the words exactly the way the character would say them. Listen to the tape or have some of your friends listen to it to see if you are expressing the feelings, paying attention to the punctuation marks, reading at an appropriate rate, saying each word clearly, and reading smoothly.

1. Jane was excited! It was Saturday and she was going to go ride go-carts with her friend, Tina. Oh how she had waited for this day! She could picture herself pushing the gas pedal all the way down. Jane especially liked to go around the corners quickly. She knew she would be able to beat Tina.

2. Sherry was angry! Every day she was blamed for things her little sister did. She was tired of hearing her mother yell at her for things she did not do. Just then she heard her mother say, "Who left the towels on the bathroom floor?" Sherry's sister answered immediately by saying, "I didn't do it." Sherry's mother began to yell, "If I've told you once, I've told you a

million times not to leave towels on the floor!" Sherry covered her ears with her hands and said under her breath, "I am running away."

3. Jimmy hated to get up! Today was the day he had dreaded for a long time. Science reports were due and he had not even begun his. He simply did not know how to make a report. He told his mother he was sick, but she didn't believe him. She told him to go to school and see how he felt. As he walked through the door he did not even say good morning to his teacher. He knew he was in for trouble.

4. It was a sad day for the Johnsons. When they were out shopping in the afternoon, someone robbed their house. The television, the tape recorder, and everyone's banks were stolen. They called the police, but the police said they probably would not get their things back. Unfortunately, the Johnsons did not have any insurance. They all sat around and wondered what they could do now.

From *A Reading Skillbuilder: Comprehension* © 1982 by Scott, Foresman & Co. Harry W. Forgan and Bonnie F. Striebel

# Reading with Your Child

Dear Parents,

My teacher wants you to read with me to help me become a better reader. Will you read this list of suggestions and read a book with me? Thanks.

From *A Reading Skillbuilder: Comprehension* © 1982 by Scott, Foresman & Co.
Harry W. Forgan and Bonnie F. Striebel

1. Try to read with your child at least four times a week for about 15–20 minutes. Some children and parents like to read together after supper, while others enjoy reading before bedtime. Set aside a *specific* time so that reading together becomes a part of your routine. Fathers should do this too!

2. Make sure you get books your child can read successfully. If your child misses more than one out of twenty words on an average, the book is too difficult. You may want to read more difficult books to your child, but do not expect children to read them because they want to show you how well they can read.

3. Alternate reading every other page or every few pages. Make sure your child has an opportunity to listen to your model as an experienced oral reader. This also gives your child a chance to rest and enjoy the story.

4. If you are reading with your child and the child comes to an unknown word, you should pronounce the word. Do not take time to have the child sound out the word or try to guess what it is. This usually interrupts the meaningful and pleasurable process of reading. After you have finished the story, you can go back to the unknown words and teach them.

5. Praise your child while he or she is reading. Be specific when you praise by pointing out a particular word the child recognized, the way the child read with expression, the child's answer to a question, and so forth.

6. Discuss the story as you go along. Remember, the emphasis should be on getting the meaning rather than on recognizing the words. Do not hesitate to point out the meanings of words that may be unfamiliar by giving a simple synonym that the child knows. Also discuss some of the pictures and use them to increase the child's understanding.

7. Make sure you stop reading together before the child is tired. It is best to stop an activity when it is most enjoyable rather than to continue to the point of boredom.